Pray for Joy

PRAY
FOR
JOY

by

Martin H. Franzmann

CONCORDIA PUBLISHING HOUSE
ST. LOUIS   LONDON

Concordia Publishing House, St. Louis, Missouri
Concordia Publishing House Ltd., London, E. C. 1
Copyright © 1970 by Concordia Publishing House
Library of Congress Catalog Card No 73-98298

MANUFACTURED IN THE UNITED STATES OF AMERICA

Contents

Preface

Publishing one's prayers comes dangerously close to praying at street corners to be seen by men. I hope the users of this book will put a more charitable construction on this publication and consider it an attempt to help others toward fulfilling the apostolic injunction to "pray constantly" and to "give thanks in all circumstances," even in some of the less likely and obvious ones. This is "the will of God in Christ Jesus" for us all and, as I have found, a great help toward fulfilling that injunction which for us melancholy myopics of the 1970s is the most difficult of all: "Rejoice always."

Martin H. Franzmann

Praise for the Sureness of God's Gifts

How sure, how sure
   the unbent and unending
      circling of the lights
     which Your primeval Word
      has coiled around my world!
How sure
   the fixed procession
    of my days and nights,
   the ordered cadence
    of the seasons,
   and the counted rhythm
    of my lapsing years!
Nothing more sure than these,
nothing more sure
   than the fixed dying
     they dole out to me—
      save You.

Only Your giving is more sure than they.
Only the life You give us
   will outlast and outshine them all.

To Find Joy in Life's Trials

You put me on the stretch, O God.
You do me the honor of putting me to the test
    as You once tested our father Abraham.
You bid me do the impossible:
    not only to endure
        the tempering heat of trial
    but to rejoice in it—impossible!

But Your Son did not find it impossible
    when You tried Him with failure.
He rejoiced in the Holy Spirit
    and gave thanks to You
when You took from Him
    the wise and understanding
and revealed Him only to babes,
    to the inconsequential little ones
        in whom Your love delights.

Your servant Paul found it possible.
Your servant James found it possible.
And You are my Father just as You are theirs.

12

I thank You for all proofs of Fatherhood.
I thank You for the trials I meet.
Give me the heart
  to meet them unafraid,
  to joy in them as I rejoice in You.

Thanks for Harsh Medicine

O Lord of Hosts,
You have bedeviled us,
    and Satan's leash seems longer
        than it used to be.
You have taken
    all the dash and gallantry
        out of war.
There are no longer
    any wars to read about,
    wars to discuss.

We are all sitting
        in one another's laps,
    and there is blood
        on all our hands.
Every shot fired anywhere
    is aimed at all of us:
        a shot fired in Biafra
        nicks the Washington Monument
        and ricochets
        round Trafalgar Square.

We are hard put to find
   a cleanly righteous cause.
We are always fighting wars
   we know no one will ever win,
   wars it does not pay to fight.
And millions watch their butter—
   if they know what butter is—
      go up in acrid smoke
      or plummet earthward
      in a packaged hell.

All who take the sword
   will perish by the sword.
We know now,
   sobered by Your medicine:
Your Son, our Lord, spoke truth;
   wars are the key signature
      of our perishing world.
And we must wait
   and hope
   and pray,
      "Thy kingdom come!"

For a Living Hope

O God,
You have given Your people
   a future and a hope—
hope fixed and grounded
   in the resurrection of Your Son,
who lives and reigns,
who by His Spirit has given us
   a vision that can look
      beyond the gray breakers
        of our successive days
      and through the mists
        that obscure Your sun,
   out to the quiet shore
      of our unending home with You.

Oh, keep us in that hope, that vision.
Let us not lose it
   amid the clutter of the things
      that we possess,
   that threaten ever and again
      to possess us.

Teach us the loose hold
    on Your present gifts
        lest we lose the greater gifts
            You hold in store.

Teach us to hold to that hope
    even amid our good and pure concern
        for this world's agonies
lest we forget
    that we can do no more
        than bind up this world's wounds
            until Your Son returns
        and lifts up finally
            the fallen world;
lest we forget
    that this hope
        is the most precious thing
            that we can give to men;
lest we forget
    that giving mammon
        is no cure for hopelessness,
    that hopeless men well housed
        are hopeless still,
    that men fed on our food
        are futureless
            for all our feeding them.

And since we are men who go
    from far left to extreme right,
    from one ditch to the other,

and cannot hold a true course
    down the road
        that leads homeward,
let us not use our hope to shield us
    from the poor who cry to us,
    the poor in whose
        outstretched hands
        and upturned faces
           we can see
the hands and face of Jesus Christ,
    who at the last will come to judge us all.
Through Him we pray.

On a Rainy Day

O Lord,
according to my definition
      of good weather
   this is not a good day:
The world is flat gray-green
   and discouraged brown.
The trees drip.
And the houses hunch up
   their slate shoulders
      against the wet.
There is only
   a shallow sky to look up to,
      smeared with rag ends of cloud.
And my feet are dampish.
And the bottoms of my trousers
   cling dankly to my ankles.
And every building I go into
   smells of wet cloth.
And people don't look
   very good to me either,
      today.

Forgive me, Lord, this insolence
that puts me
    at the center of the universe
  and makes me
    judge of all things,
      including Your weather;
that blinds me
  to Your steady benevolence
    towards us,
    the ungrateful and the evil;
that makes me impatient
  with this gracious saturation,
  this liquid life that overruns the world,
  this clean cadence of fertility,
  this cool caress of water on my cheek,
  this silver spread on streets,
  this mirroring transfiguration
    of our pavements.

Why, it's a great day, Lord.
I thank You.

For Help in Temptation

"The woman whom Thou gavest
        to be with me,"
    Adam said,
"she gave me fruit of the tree,
    and I did eat."
We are born Adam's sons
    and go his way
        of easy accusation
            of the Lord, our God.

O God,
You sent Your Son
    to turn us back
        from Adam's sins
        and Adam's death.
You sent Him
        into Adam's dying
            for our sake
    that we might live,
        no longer Adam's sons
            but Yours.

Give us the Spirit Your Son has promised us,
    to make us honest men again,
    to know and face the truth,
    to see ourselves and cease
    from laying our defections
        at Your door;
to see Your only goodness in Your Word
    and in our desperate need of You.

To Forget Past Sins

O God,
You have trodden
     our iniquities underfoot
  and have cast
    all our sins
       into the depths of the sea.
You have forgotten
  as You have forgiven.
The rising sun is not darkened
  by my dark yesterday;
my hot rebellion of yesteryear
  has not dried
    this year's compassionate rain
  or parched the teeming earth
    on which I walk.

Oh, still this guilty memory of mine,
  this dark and unadmitted doubt of You,
    this questioning
      of Your forgiveness
      and Your forgetting.

Oh, do not let them rise again to torment me,
    those harsh defacements of my fellowman,
    those words that flew,
        arrows fiery with my anger,
    those proud and brittle clashes
        of me against my neighbor,
    those ragged neglects of simple duty.

Your Son's cross stands empty against the sky.
    Your Son's grave is opened wide.
        Your angels have spoken.
And Your Son sits at Your right hand
    for me, for me.

Let me remember this;
    let me forget.

Joy in the Gift of Exaltation

You have given us wisdom,
    O Giver God;
You have taken from us our trust
    in the solid durability of wealth.
You have stripped us down to beggarhood.

But what a fine lot of beggars we are:
beggars on horseback,
    riding high,
    riding toward Your eternal city,
      with spurs that jingle hope,
      and accoutrements that rattle confidence,
    riding on horses whose hoofbeats
        hammer out our exaltation on the road.

O Giver,
    O Captain,
        O King of all us beggar-kings,
Yours is the glory forever and forever.

That the Word
May Work in Us

O God, almighty and all-merciful,
once chaos gave way
    before Your command,
and Your creation stood forth
        structured, wonderful,
    to call forth melody
        from all the singing stars.

Our wild rebellion
    shivered and blackened all that,
    called a chaos down
        more fearful than the first;
and You have spoken
    a Word more powerful,
    Your Word of love,
        Your Son,
and You have made us —
    ah, gift intolerable —
        the firstfruits
            of Your new and righteous world.
You have made us sons.

Ah, gift intolerable—
    how shall we show forth
        the splendor of the world to come,
        the home of righteousness
            which shall one day live here
                unbroken and entire?
We cannot—but Your Word can.

Oh, let it work in us,
    that Word implanted in our midst,
    Your creative Word,
and let us bring forth summer fruits for You.

To Live by the Word of God

O Lord,
we are men of flickering faith;
we do not have the courage
    to put You to the test,
    to take You at Your word,
    to give You what is Yours,
that You may open the windows of heaven
    and pour down on us
        Your overflowing blessing;
we doubt that Your heart
        is as great and good
    as Your strong Word
        would make us believe,
that the riches of Your glory in Christ Jesus
    will supply our every need.

O Lord,
we are men of half faith,
    of cloven faith,
        half given to You,
        half saved up for ourselves,

faith that would tempt You,
   experiment with You,
   use You
      to entrench us in our ways,
      to serve our ends,
      to give us greater greatness
         than You have given us
            when You made us sons of God.

Forgive us, Lord.
Teach us, O Lord.
Let Your Spirit blow
   and make our faith burn
      steady and clear,
   a flame upon Your altar;
let Your Spirit
   make our believing whole
   and wholly sane,
      a monomania of trust in You,
      merely suspended
         from Your high sustaining Word.

Teach us to walk
      as Your Son walked on the earth
   through ministry to death,
   through death to life and glory
      at Your right hand.
Through Him we pray.

For the Consecration of Sex

O good Creator,
You made us man and woman;
You blessed us in our being
    for each other;
You planted Your creative potency in us
    and bound us to each other
        with seeking coquetry
            and the gallantry of proud pursuit,
        with living tendrils of delight,
        with new life, radiant,
            of our bodies sprung.

Forgive us, Lord.
We have forgotten Eden
    and have run from You
        down darkling paths
            of selfishness.
We have defiled Your gift
    and held cheap Your blessing.
We have made a mania of Your gift
    of conjugal sanity.

Bless us again, we pray,
through Jesus Christ,
who smiled on us
at Cana once.

Thanksgiving for
the Pure Pleasure of Motion

When I was a boy,
   O Lord,
I used to run
   through the beautiful world
     You gave me to move in.
I skipped on concrete walks,
   dogtrotted down dusty country roads,
     dashed through cold creeks,
scrambled through brush,
   up narrow hill paths,
crawled up shelved cliffs
   overlooking the river,
scuffed through fallen leaves,
   swished through dead grasses,
     slithered through greasy-soft mud,
pumped through drifted snow,
   clonked over hollow ice —
     oh, it was great, Lord.
And I thank You
   for the memory
     of those brute-rapid happy days.

I move more slowly now
    on long, deliberate walks.
I look more
    at the sky and the clouds above me,
    at the swirling machinery of traffic,
    at the architecture of an ordered world
as my legs take over and ignore me,
    moving on a rhythm
        deeper than my consciousness.
Oh, this wonderful,
    this milder motion,
that moves more narrowly
    and takes in more
        than that first
            breathless race of mine!

What a river to walk by,
    these eddies of people —
boys, girls,
    laughing, whistling,
    calling, screaming,
    beautiful in their
        unconscious comeliness
            of ceaseless motion;
girls growing womanly;
boys shambling
    in first awkward manliness,
        flamboyant and unafraid;
nurses padding by
    in their flat-footed, easy grace;

young mothers with their babies
    riding on their hips;
good, solid mothers
    carrying big, brown bags;
old women,
    wrinkled, white,
    fulfilled, serene,
    living out
        the last quiet measures
            of the eternal song;
and all these men,
    each one a man,
        one of a kind —
how can I begin to praise
    this crazy aggregate
        of amazing bipeds
    under this sky,
        clear, bright,
        subdued, lowering,
        flat-gray, cloud-heaped,
        wind-pummeled,
            never the same on any Tuesday?

You have made all things beautiful
    in their season,
not least the varied motions of a man
    as he lives longer
        and grows older.
For this I thank You.

In an Art Gallery

This is uncanny, Lord:
    a rutted sandy road
        running through grass
            to a railroad crossing,
    a semaphore
        against a blue sky
        and a white cloud,
    a little water color
        on a piece of rough paper.
I've seen this all a thousand times,
    but here it is,
        trapped and alive and held:
the golden blue of every glorious summer day,
the everlasting simple grass and sand and sky,
    a bit of the first morning,
        when the morning stars sang together
            and the sons of God shouted for joy.
Adam could walk across this railroad track,
and Eve, still nude and unashamed.
    Uncanny is hardly the word for it;
        call it Your miracle.

I thank You, Lord,
    for the miracle
        of this artist's eye of innocence,
    this deep adoration of Your handiwork
that lets me look upon Your world again
    as once Your Son could look
        on lilies of the field
            growing in Galilee.

For Busy People

O Lord,
Your Son,
the Son of Man
      for us men for our salvation,
   had not where to lay His head
     when foxes found their dens
     and the birds of heaven
        settled rustling to their nests.

Your servant Paul
   spent and was spent,
      ground fine between the turning wheels
        of the business of his Lord.

We thank You, Lord,
   for busy people everywhere:
those fine, long ranks of men of conscience
   who march straight and steady
      on the business of Your world
   and live on the small, gray satisfaction
      of their work well done.

How good they are, these devotees of duty!
What a piece of work
    is the working of Your will
        in their wills!
Work gets done. Contracts are fulfilled.
Buses and trains and planes arrive on time.
Letters get delivered.
My morning papers and my milk are at my door.
Roads are repaired, streets are swept.
Lighthouses wink steadily
    through the unwatched hours.

How good they are!
How much more beautiful
    than the colorful idlers,
    the coffee-sipping critics of the humdrum,
    the dreamy rebels,
        who would be up to their necks
            in their own rubbish
but for the unfailing ministrations
    of those colorless consciences they despise!

Forgive me, Lord,
for taking them for granted,
for putting on them leisurely demands
    for more and more,
for blanking out their persons
    with some utilitarian, impersonal,
        covering epithet
            like "service personnel."

Remember them in mercy, O Lord.
Give them joy in the jobs they do so well.
Give them eyes to see
    the greatness of the ordered world
        which they keep orderly — for You.
Let them not grow small
        in listless littleness of heart;
    nor smug in their own decency;
    nor hard on those
        who seem less busy than themselves;
    nor forgetful, in their harassments, of You,
        too busy for the blessing of Your Word,
        too preoccupied to walk
            through the gate of prayer
                which You hold open to us all.

For Young People

O Lord,
You have made the young so beautiful;
    even their awkwardness has in it
        a grace we delight to see.
Their easy, never-ending laughter,
    their rippling, eddying energy —
        they amaze us still
        and stir us strangely
with memories of half-forgotten freedoms,
    of unsagging drives of constant power;
with memories of a time
    when we did not need
        to portion out our efforts
            and ration our spurts.

We thank You
    for the beauty they bring
        into our ebbing days,
    for the memories they quicken,
    for the promise
        that their simply being speaks.

Surely You have not written off a world
    that has such power and beauty in it.
You have not said no to man
    when he can live anew,
        so mightily and freshly,
            in his children.
We cannot call them ours
    because we begot them
    and bore them;
You have created them,
and You will bless them,
and You will bless the world
    that is their home,
and You will bless us through them too.

O Lord, there they are, the young:
so vulnerable,
so liable to hurt,
so prone to injury,
so open to the backlash of melancholy
    and melancholy's close cousin:
        self-pity;
so prone to draw in upon themselves,
    to think themselves
        a kind and class apart,
    to distrust and ignore
        all ages but their own;
so intent on gulping experience,
    all experience,
        any experience;

so eager to shed the innocence
    that is their one-time,
        one-time-only glory;
so bent on a sophistication
    they will find too dearly bought;
so impatient to have done with,
    to have lost
        what a man can never find again
          all his days.

O Lord,
give us grace to love them
    when they irritate us most;
give us wisdom,
give us Your Spirit,
give us words
    that will not stop
        at their ears.

O Lord, by us
    or by whatever secret ways You have,
teach them to take delight in the walls
    which our love and Yours have built
        to trap the sunlight for them,
        the sunlight young plants need;
teach them to value love
    in all its forms,
    in all the sterner ways
        that love must go
          if it be love indeed;

teach them to know the love
    that lives and works
        in discipline,
        in the clear cup
            of tradition's wholesome drink,
        in measure and restraint,
        in the settled comeliness
            of courteous form.

O Lord, forgive them
    the unconscious harshness
        of their willful ways.
Take them up
    into Your kind, almighty hands.
Bless them and keep them.
Let their quick devotion be acceptable:
    a morning scent,
    an easy song,
    an improvised and unrepeatable melody
        to Your glory.

To Respect Language

O good Creator,
O Judge of the world,
    You left us long reminders,
        after the Fall,
    in the midst of the world's futility,
of that far-off, that very good creation
    which Your Word called out of chaos
        and adorned with marshaled loveliness
        for our delight.

Even after Babel
    You have left on human words
        the imprint of Your will
that the family of man
    should live in colloquy
    and one day speak Your name together.
You have put the promise of Pentecost
    on our speech.
And Your Son has put upon our every word,
        our every idle word,
    the accent of accountability.

O Judge of all our words,
wipe clean the slate,
wipe out the record
    of that fearful debt
        which idle words have written.
Teach us once more to speak,
        under the sky
            of Your forgiving love,
    as men made in Your image
        ought to speak,
    as men for whose redemption
            the Word went into death
        should speak,
    as men tongued with the Spirit's fire
        ought to speak,
treasuring the gift
    of articulateness,
    of lucid commerce
        with You, with men.

Strip from our words
    the trashy tinsel,
    the seductive streamers
        of our expert propaganda.
Quench the coruscations
    of our treasured wrath.
Put away the measured meanness
    of our contempt.
Silence the sodden measures
    of our cheap sentiments.

Let our words be clean
      and fresh
      and strong
         with paradisal innocence.
Let them be human words again,
      worthy of man,
      worthy of You, O Son of Man,
         who once shared with us,
         familiarly, our speech.

A Prayer for Wisdom

We turn a corner
    and stagger at the unexpected wind
        that sweeps our street.
We look fearfully
    into the shadowy corners
        and dark doorways
    and complain
        of the inadequate lighting
           of our streets.
We step fretfully across puddles.
We fuss and fret our way through mud—
    as if we were alone,
    as if You were gone,
        an absentee God
           careless of His own.

O Lord,
give us light
    to see You steadily
    and see You whole
        in all Your world;

give us wisdom
    to fear
    and to obey
    and trust
the God unseen whom we can see,
O God made visible by Your own illumining,
    to trust You
        round all corners,
        down all streets,
        in all shadows,
        across all puddles,
        through all mud,
in Your world,
    ruled by Your almighty and all-giving hand,
        through Jesus Christ our Lord.

Thanks for the Beginning of Wisdom

O God of wisdom immeasurable,
we have heaped up knowledge,
    sacked it,
    packed it in,
    and stacked it,
    reared it in towers
        that scratch Your sky,
    sorted it out judiciously,
    classified it nicely,
    disposed it over surfaces,
    on ground that quakes beneath us.

What are we, then?
Where are we now?
At best, perched on boughs of indecision
    or huddled in nests of resignation;
at worst, fluttering and hysterical,
    screaming a protest
    or singing flat songs
        of hopelessness
            in a hopeful key.

What a book *In Praise of Folly*
  some cool-hearted wag could write of us
if anyone had the courage still
  to play court jester to the King of kings!

Where shall wisdom be found . . . ?
Man does not know the way to it,
and it is not found in the land of the living.
  We know that now.

God understands the way to it. . . .
And He said to man,
"Behold, the fear of the Lord, that is wisdom."
  You have taught us that.

O God of immeasurable goodness,
You have given Your Son to be for us
    the power of God and the wisdom of God.
  For this we humbly thank You.

Oh, give us fear to bow before Him
  in His foolish majesty
and learn a wisdom
  that will stand the shocks of the world
and come through the crash
  and the howling
      of the end of the world.

To Be Rid of Some
Current and Popular Illusions

Rid us, O Lord,
    of the arrogant delusion
that our age is
    harder to live in,
    harder to live through
    and be decent in
        than any age
            that ever was,
that we are being tried
    as our fathers never were,
that we have more excuse
    for our neurotic screaming,
    our pitiful muddling,
    our eroded standards,
    our sentimental slobbering,
    our pinching terror
        at the shadows of the future
        cast upon our way
    than any men who ever walked
        beneath Your heaven
        and on Your earth.

Teach us, O Lord,
      by Your sane and steadying Word
that we stand before You
            as we always stood,
      living of Your grace
      and moving toward Your judgment,
that the Bomb
and the terrible technological trifles
            of our time
      have not altered
            the great,
            plain,
            steady fact
that You are Lord
      and have not changed
            the blessed time
                  of Your coming
                        as a thief in the night.

While Reading the News

O God Almighty,
I thank You
    for this net that sweeps all waters
    and brings me news of all the daily life
        of all my neighbors
           everywhere in the world.
Make me compassionate,
        O God of all mercies,
    with all my neighbors' sufferings.

Teach me to know and feel
    that distant anguish is
        as aching as my own.
Teach me to pray,
    "Thy kingdom come!"
        as widely as Your Son
           has willed it and meant it.
Teach me to do
    what I can and must do
        for all men.
Teach me long-reaching charity.

Give me faith to know,
    when news is black as ink,
that Your hand is guiding all,
    obscurely and unfathomably
        but surely, surely
            toward Your goal;
that when the world shakes
and Satan triumphs with short certainty,
    Your Son, Jesus Christ, is Lord of all,
that He, the Lamb slain for our sins,
    is opening the seals of Your book
    and is working out
        Your good and holy will.

Remember in Your mercy
    the gatherers and disseminators of the news.
Protect them from all harm.
Keep them
    from cynical and cheap success,
    from a single taste for disaster,
    from unconsidered or deliberate distortion
        of the sad and wondrous face of man.

In a Democracy

Almighty Ruler of us all,
you have made us to be
    both Caesar
    and Caesar's subjects.
You have given us,
    wrapped in the blessing
      of the free,
        this dual and difficult
          duty to fulfill.

Give us the meekness of wisdom to know
    that the good laws we make
      are not our laws simply
        to do with as we please
      but have upon them
        Your hallowed instancy,
        Your inviolable majesty;
    that when we make and honor bad laws,
      we are flouting You, the Righteous,
      and You will visit on us
        our unfaithfulness.

55

Teach us to know
    that the men we have elected
      are Your instruments,
      with Your sword in their hands.
Teach us to bow
    before Your majesty
      hid in such deep disguise.

For Men in Protest

O furious Cleanser
　　of the house of God,
O Blaster of the fruitless tree,
look in mercy on these men
　　whose love compels them
　　　　to spell out in act
their anguished impatience
　　at the sloth of law,
their no to legal illegalities,
their militant compassion
　　for the wronged
　　and all the nameless,
　　　　faceless
　　　　　　poor and dispossessed.
Keep them from intoxication
　　with their rightness.

Give them charity toward those
　　who cannot be as militant as they,
　　who walk down other, longer roads
　　　　toward the same goal.

Preserve them from driving
　　　the wedge of power
　so deep into the grain
　　　　of structured equity
　　that all goes crashing.
Bid them guard with care the flame
　　that breaks so quickly into a fire
that makes an indifferent holocaust
　　of all the works
　　　　of Your judicial hand.
Lord, give us all
　　a heart of quick compassion,
　　wisdom to plan and execute
before the too-late of our action
　　　　breeds the swarms of scorpions
　　whose sting shall make us all
　　　　long for death we cannot find.

For Charity
Toward Men in Office

Almighty God,
You have ordained the authorities that are;
You have clothed them in a majesty
    that is higher and stronger
    than the given facts of their history,
a majesty that wakens fear in us
    and claims honor from us.

O God, remember in Your mercy
    the men who bear the burden of this majesty,
    men like us, easily bent
        by the pressure of temptation,
        by the impact of expediency.
Remember them and strengthen them
        when they are moved
    to shade the truth to their own ends,
    to withhold what should be told,
    to distort what must be told,
    to disclose what does not serve
        our common weal.
Keep intact their honor and their credibility.

Purge us, O God,
   of cynical distrust,
   of party passion,
   of the deafness
      of our rebellious bent.
Teach us, O Lord, the meekness
   that would rather be deceived
      than be encrusted
         with perpetual distrust.
Teach the charity
   that will interpret
      all uncertainties
         toward the side of goodness.
Create in our world
   an air in which
      the truth can freely breathe,
   a sea on which
      the ships of truth can sail,
   an earth on which
      the feet of truth can walk unhurt.

Your Son, our Lord,
   would not speak ill of Caesar
      even when Caesar's power
         nailed Him to the cross.
Give us the Spirit of Your Son.

For the Police

O Lord, I thank You
for the mighty and intricate
        machine of justice
    Your Law has fashioned
        for my good,
the elaborate and vigilant network
    of men and instruments
        that think and prowl
            and click and calculate
that I may move,
    secure and peaceable,
        on pleasant paths
            of ordered decency.

Remember in mercy, O Lord,
    the men who stand between me
        and the chaos of bestial lawlessness.
Give them, O Lord,
awareness of the high majesty of the law
    which clothes their work and them
        with awesome dignity;

patience to bear the conspicuous loneliness
        of men in uniform
    and to endure the slick disdain
        that falls on all
            embodiments of rectitude;
strength to resist the corrosive wash
    of the temptations
        that are peculiarly theirs:
to grow harsh in the face of brutality,
    vindictive in the face of endless malice;
to make the easy, cynical, venal compromise
    with small-scale wrong
        that does not seem to matter much;
to settle into dark contempt
    of the mankind
        whose unlovely features
            are continually before their eyes.

O Lord,
let all good men hear ever and again
    the thundering voice
        of unendurable Sinai,
and let them look
        with new, respectful eyes,
    ever and again,
    on the men,
    the plain, frail men,
        whose daily work articulates for us
            the far-off voice of Sinai.

To Love the Law

Your Law, O Lord,
   written on men's hearts,
   inscribed and learned
     by multitudes of men,
   seeping through a thousand crevices
     into the remote corners
       of our world—
Your Law has reared
not only the huge symmetries of justice,
   those marred majesties,
but even these little
     complexities of discipline
   that make the grit of life
     less grinding,
   the collision of will on will
     less violent:
yellow lines on roads,
meters on the curb,
patrol boys at crossings,
lights that guide us with bright control
or blinking warn us in our hastiness.

Teach us, O Lord,
to see in them a refraction from flashing Sinai,
to see Your moving finger in their work,
to give them our ready and quick assent,
to delight in them
    as men made new
        in Your Son Jesus Christ, our Lord.
Through Him we pray.

While Driving

A great thing, Lord,
this pride of lions,
   herd of horses,
      aerie of eagles,
this eater-up of miles,
   this saver of minutes,
      this runner of errands,
this purring bearer
     of burdens,
   this expediter
       of the tediously necessary,
   this speeder
     toward the countryside,
this expander of my horizon,
   this smooth responder
     to my guiding hand
     and my controlling foot.
A great thing,
a good gift,
a thing to be treasured,
   and to be feared —

Oh, make and keep it
   good and useful
      in my hands.
Oh, keep my hands and eyes
   alert and sure.
Keep my mind clear,
my heart responsive
   to the trust You put in me
      when You gave this gift
         of leashed and concentrated power.
Let it not be for mischief in my hands.
Let me in this and all things honor You.

For the Slob

O Lord,
You have loved us all to the death
and have bidden us love all men,
 not all men on principle
  and in general
 but each man personally
  and in particular.
And that is hard.

It is hard, O Lord,
 to enter into that freedom
  from ourselves and for each other,
 the freedom that makes all other liberty
  look like a cheap half-holiday
   on a cluttered beach.

And the hardest of all to love is the slob,
who claims to be as good as anybody
  (a proposition we are not par-
  ticularly interested in arguing
  until *he* lays it on the table)

and proceeds to prove,
      dramatically and in detail,
   that he is inferior to almost everybody.
There he is, there he sits,
   like dirty dishes on the table of mankind,
      left over from a meal two hours ago.

It is hard, O Lord,
   to feel any feeling
   stronger than disgust for him.
He flouts the common decencies
   that make us chipped
      and tarnished creatures
    of Your grace tolerable to each other.
He litters Your clean woodlands
   and spits into the clear springs
      You have made to issue
       from Your pure and ancient rocks.
He roars, an instrument of fatal malice,
      down the roads
   which long centuries of communal decencies
    have worn into a pleasant pattern
      on the traveled earth.
He makes streets rustle
   with the dry rasp of his discarded cartons
      and stink with his uneaten superfluities.
He scrawls vulgarities
   and obscenities
   and homosexually coy indecencies
      on clean and useful washroom walls.

He cumulatively mounts the decibels
        of his half-idiot music
    till the world grows poor
        in the silences that save our sanity,
    until there is no room for saner melody.
And worst of all:
he wears the cast-off clothing of romance
and pipes a lean and flashy siren song
    that makes the feet of human mice,
        poor gray things,
    and the feet of rebel children,
        young and not so young,
    tingle to trot his path of dubious liberty.

O Lord, how shall we love him?
And yet, under the wide compulsion
        of Your cross,
    how shall we *not* love him?
Open our eyes, O Lord, and make us see
    the cruel consequences of our soft contempt
        that has left vacuums his noise can fill.
Have we made decency a quiet club
        with a door of such formidable oak
    that such as he cannot dare
        even to knock on it?
Have we made the huge excitement of Your love
        so dull a thing
    that alcoholic raptures
    and chemical revelations of the soul
        seem to promise more?

O Lord, remember in Your mercy
    these unmerciful;
and in Your love remember
    these unlovable.
and in Your wisdom teach us,
    the unteachable:
        teach us to pray,
        teach us to love,
        teach us to say:
Thy will
    (the will that never
    shut out any slob)
        be done.

For the Grace
to Grow Old Gratefully

O God, the Savior of us all,
    when Your Son walked among us,
He looked upon and loved
    all ages of men,
    babies, children, the young,
    the mature, the aged.
He took upon Him the sins of all ages of men.
He died for us all
and rose again for all of us
    that we might all,
        each on his appointed path,
    henceforth live to Him and serve Him
        all the days of our lives.

O good Creator of us all,
You have designed all ages of man
and have put Your blessing
    on all our times and seasons.
You have made our lives a living pattern
    curiously and variously woven
        for Your glory.

You have made our lives
    an intricate instrument
        in Your cunning hand
    to play tunes
        in all keys,
        in all volumes,
        in all tempos,
            for Your praise.

O breathing Spirit, Giver of all life,
O great Revealer of all truth,
You have made young men to see visions
and old men to dream dreams.
Your Word has come to us
    spoken by young and old
    by hot, impetuous, young prophets,
    by men in the high noonday
        of their strength
    and by serene and wise old men.
Your Word has given "elder"
    a grave and honored ring
and has put honor
    on the gray-haired head
    and on the bald pate too.

Forgive us our blindness,
that we have not seen
    the light that falls
        on every inch and fraction
            of our way.

Forgive us our dullness,
that we have not known
    the long dimensions of Your bounty—
(we have dared to think that,
the gift of youth once given,
You have no further gift to give).
Forgive us our impatience,
that we have not heard You out
    beyond the first bright paragraph
            of our history—
        as if You had no further word to say.

Set us free
from our willful obsession with youth,
from our ludicrous and costly attempts
    at aping youth when youth is past,
from our distrust of You
    that makes us look backward
    only to what cannot be again,
from our slobbering, regretful tears
    that blind us to Your present love.

Teach us
to savor the blessing of each age
    as each age comes,
to forget what lies behind,
to live today,
to strain in simple confidence
    toward the hidden future
        as toward the gifts You have yet to give.

Teach us
to unlearn at least the brute heroic aim
    of girding ourselves
    and going where we would go,
to stretch out our hands
and let ourselves be led
    we know not where.

Teach us
to bless You for what You give
    and what You take away;
to accept in meekness
    our diminishing powers;
to husband shrewdly
    the energies that remain;
to use the gifts
    that only age can give;
to live and work in large sympathy
    with all generations of men,
being taught compassion and humility
    by remembered failures of our own.

Teach us
to give thanks in this our day
    for the kindly geriatric ministries
        that make our faltering lives
            more pleasurable
        and for the public conscience
            You have wakened
                to make our old age more secure

that we may use the last coins
at the bottom of the purse
in reckless fine expenditure for You;
that the concluding cadence of our life may be
a clear continuation of the song
that sounded first
when we were born,
that piped us, swaggering,
down the paths of youth,
that marched us steady
through the middle years
and can ring still—
and we may still respond:
Alleluia! Alleluia!

A Wedding Prayer

O God of Eden,
    O Christ of Cana,
        O Creator Spirit, Spirit of love,
Remember in mercy
    this Thy servant
    and this Thy handmaid.

Give them, O Father,
    under the heaven of Thy forgiveness,
        the primeval blessing
            of our garden home.

Give them, O Christ,
    Redeemer of us all,
        the bounty
            of Thy plenteous wine of joy.

Give them, O Spirit,
    the glory of the Christ
        whom Thou dost glorify.
Give them Thy gift of oneness in their Lord.

So shall they praise and bless Thee,
    Holy Trinity,
praise and bless Thee
    all the days of their life,
and join with us
    to sing Thine everlasting praise
there where our praise is perfect:
    at the high feast and wedding of the Lamb.

Over a Glass of Wine

O Giver of wine to make glad the heart of man,
O genial and generous Lord of Cana,
O Giver of wisdom and wit
    and ease and laughter with our friends,
we thank You
for the winking beauty of this glass,
for this common humorous laughter
    at our too-brittle overseriousness,
for this shedding of pretense and pose
    in the loving raillery of cordial confidence.

Give us the grace to enjoy Your good gift
    without fear
    and without excess.
And give us courage to forgo it
    when we must,
    when our own weakness
        or another's stumbling step
    makes giving up this good and wholesome gift
        something more precious
            than Your cordial wine.

Grace Before Meat

We live not, Lord, by bread alone;
Without Thy blessing bread were stone.
For bread and for Thy kindly Word
We thank and bless Thee, God, our Lord.